I'm dedicating this book to my granddaughter, Madeline, who adores puppies.

Special thanks to VIP Rescue for your hard work placing puppies and dogs into forever homes.
(Very Important Poodle Rescue)

email: <u>scottytherescuedog@gmail.com</u>
Instagram: Scottytherescuedog

Scotty Gets a Puppy

The Adventures of Scotty the Rescue Dog

Written and Illustrated by Tammi Janiga

Scotty and his buddy Pico were walking through downtown Dogedin Saturday morning. Scotty stopped dead in his tracks. "Pico, check it out! So many cute puppies available for adoption! It's practically raining puppies! Let's go inside and play with them! Want to?"

"Do you have any idea how much work you have to do with a new puppy?" said Pico. "You have to take him outside every single hour for potty training. No matter if it's raining or snowing. They need lots of food. They need fresh water every day. They need walks. They need playtime. They need snuggles."

They went inside.

Mr. Kibbles, the store manager, greeted them. "How may I help you, fellas?"

"We want to meet the new rescue puppies," said Scotty. "May I see the puppy, the color of vanilla ice cream with floppy, apricot ears?"

"Oh, you don't want that one. That puppy is a handful," chuckled Mr. Kibbles.

"Why don't you play with the brown and white puppy or the apricot one?" suggested Mr. Kibbles.

"No, I want to play with the vanilla ice cream one," said Scotty. "OK!" Mr. Kibbles picked up the puppy and put him in a playroom for Pico and Scotty. The puppy was pouncing on them and nipping at them. It was so much fun!

"I LOVE him. He has a BIG personality," said Scotty. "Well, I tried to warn you about him," said Mr. Kibbles. "He is a rascal with a capital R!" Mr. Kibbles gathered a basket of items for Scotty. Puppy food, toys, blanket, bowls, leash, collar, harness, and a portable dog kennel. "Let me know what you decide to name him, and I'll order a pet ID tag," said Mr. Kibble.

Scotty and Pico walked the puppy home. "Oh, NO!" Puppy went potty on the floor. "I told you puppies are a BIG responsibility. Why don't you set a timer? Take him outside to go potty. When he goes, reward him with a treat! You must be patient. This could take a few weeks." said Pico. "It's not his fault. He is just a puppy."

When the timer went off, Scotty took the puppy outside. He praised him joyfully when he went potty in the yard.

"OUCH! He keeps biting me with his tiny, sharp teeth." cried Scotty. "He is teething. He needs a chew toy or a dog bone," said Pico. "Mr. Kibbles warned you NOT to pick that one."

"Have you seen my socks, shoes, or my ball, Pico?" asked Scotty.

He looked everywhere. Behind the chair, in the closet, under the table, and then HOLY COW! He found all of his missing things hidden under the bed. The puppy had been collecting treasures and hiding them! "Mr. Kibbles warned you NOT to pick that one," Pico giggled.

STINKY
SOCKS

"He is so cute, I can't get mad at him," said Scotty. I'm going to teach him to fetch. And to shake. Scotty took the puppy outside and tossed the ball. Puppy just sat there and looked at him. "Go get it, boy!" cheered Scotty. Puppy just watched. "Pico, can you fetch the ball so that puppy can see how to do it?" Before long, the puppy retrieved the ball. Scotty gave him a little treat when he did.

The phone was ringing, Scotty didn't want to leave the puppy alone, but he was expecting an important call. He ran inside for one minute. When he returned, the puppy had dug holes ALL OVER the yard. The puppy was FILTHY! What a mess! Scotty took the puppy inside for a bubble bath. Pico is laughing out loud. "Mr. Kibbles warned you NOT to pick that one!"

Scotty fell asleep under a shade tree and took a little nap. He woke up to puppy growling and shaking a pillow. There were feathers EVERYWHERE! What a mess. "Maybe you should keep the puppy in a kennel or a gated room when you can't supervise him," suggested Pico. The puppy is WILD and full of energy. He needs a walk. Scotty grabbed the puppies leash and harness only to discover he had chewed them to bits.

"Mr. Kibbles tried to tell you NOT to pick that one!" chuckled Pico.

The new puppy wants to play all day long.

He will sleep well tonight.

Or maybe not.

"Have you decided what to name him, Scotty" asked Pico? Puppy greets me with bear hugs when I come home. I think I'll name him Teddy. I'll call him Teddy Bear! I know he is a lot of work now, but if I take the time to train him correctly, he will prove to be an excellent family member. He is precious, and I wouldn't trade him for anything in the whole wide world. Mr. Kibbles was wrong. Teddy is pawsitively, perfect.

The End

Scotty did it again! He hid a dog bone on every picture! Can you find them?